SUPER SCIENTISTS

MARIE CURIE

Sarah Ridley

W
FRANKLIN WATTS
LONDON • SYDNEY

> "Nothing in life is to be feared,
> it is only to be understood.
> Now is the time to understand more,
> so that we may fear less."
> – *Marie Curie*

First published in 2014
by Franklin Watts

Franklin Watts
338 Euston Road
London NW1 3BH

Franklin Watts Australia
Level 17/207 Kent Street
Sydney, NSW 2000

Editor in Chief: John C. Miles
Design: Jonathan Hair and Matt Lilly
Art Director: Peter Scoulding
Picture Research: Diana Morris
Original design concept: Sophie Williams

Picture credits: ARPL/HIP/Topfoto: 8. The Granger Collection/
Topfoto: 17, 22. itsmejust/Shutterstock: front cover cr. Kaspri/
Shutterstock: front cover tr. Look and Learn: 15. Oxford
Science Archive/HIP/Topfoto: 11. Picturepoint/Topfoto:
23. Popperfoto/Getty images: 19. Roger-Viollet/Topfoto: 1,
12, 13, 14, 16, 20. Topfoto: 10. Vitalyedysh/Dreamstime: 9.
Warczakoski/Dreamstime: 5. CC Wikipedia: front cover cl, front
cover c, World History Archive/Topfoto: 4, 6, 7, 18, 21.

Dewey number 540.9'2
Hardback ISBN 978 1 4451 3061 3
Library eBook ISBN 978 1 4451 3062 0

Printed in China

Franklin Watts is a division of Hachette Children's Books,
an Hachette UK company.

www.hachette.co.uk

Contents

Childhood   4

Education and beyond   6

To university   8

Love and marriage   10

Invisible rays   12

Discovery!   14

Nobel Prize and tragedy   16

War work   18

Fund-raising trips   20

Her name lives on   22

Glossary/Index   24

Childhood

Marie Curie was born in Warsaw, Poland, in 1867. Known then as Maria Sklodowska, she was the youngest of five children. Her parents were teachers who inspired their children to work hard and ask questions.

The Curie children (from left to right): Zosia, Hela, Marie, Joseph and Bronia.

1867–1877

Marie's family lived in a flat in this Warsaw building, now a museum about Marie Curie.

7 November 1867

Marie is born.

1872

Marie's mother catches tuberculosis and has to spend time away from her children.

1873

Marie begins at primary school.

1876

Marie's eldest sister, Zosia, dies of typhus.

It was very difficult for Polish people at this time as Poland was under Russian rule. Even though it was against the law, Marie's parents taught their children the language and history of Poland.

Education and beyond

When Marie was eleven, her mother died, leaving her father to care for the family. That same year Marie started secondary school. By the time she left school at the age of fifteen, she was top of the class, winning a gold medal.

Marie's mother had to keep away from her children as much as possible, to avoid passing on her illness – tuberculosis.

1878	**1878**	**1883**
Marie's mother dies of tuberculosis.	Marie starts secondary school, developing a passion for science.	Marie leaves school, top of the class. She spends a year living with cousins in the countryside.

Marie worked as a governess, teaching the children of the family who lived in this house.

Girls were not allowed to go to university in Poland so Marie and her sister, Bronia, came up with a plan. Marie decided to work as a governess for a farming family, sending her wages to support Bronia while she studied to become a doctor in France. In return, Bronia would help Marie to study once she had become a doctor.

1884

Marie and Bronia study at secret classes in Warsaw.

1886–1889

Marie works as a governess, falls in love with her employer's son and runs a free school for country children.

To university

1889

Marie returns to Warsaw to live with her father.

1891

Aged 24, she moves to Paris to study at the Sorbonne. This is when she changes her name from Maria to Marie.

1893

She gains the top mark at the university in physics.

1894

She studies for a maths degree.

After three years, Marie returned to Warsaw to live with her father. She took a new job as a governess and spent time experimenting with science at a secret laboratory in Warsaw. Eventually she was ready to leave Poland for university in France.

This photo, dated 1890, shows Marie's father with his daughters: Marie, Bronia and Hela.

1889–1894

Marie studied at the Sorbonne in Paris, France, still a world-famous university.

At first Marie lived with her sister Bronia, now married to a doctor. Soon she decided to rent a student room where she could study harder. Even though she had little money for food or fun she finished her degree in physics with the top mark. Soon she started a second degree in maths.

BREAKTHROUGH

Marie achieved the top mark in her year for her physics degree. So few women studied at university in the 1890s that this was a huge achievement. She went on to be the first woman in Europe to gain a doctorate in science in 1903.

Love and marriage

Marie needed money to support her student life so she took a job in a laboratory, working on magnets. Here she met Pierre Curie, a tall, young scientist who was eight years older than her. They fell in love and were married in 1895.

Pierre and Marie spent their honeymoon cycling around the countryside.

1894

She works in a laboratory, studies maths at university and meets Pierre Curie.

1895

She marries Pierre.

1895

Wilhelm Rontgen discovers X-rays.

1894–1897

Marie and Pierre with their daughter, Irene.

The Curies shared a love for each other and for science. Marie continued to work on magnets and published her first scientific work on this subject soon after her daughter, Irene, was born in 1897. Pierre's father moved in to help raise the baby.

1896

Henri Becquerel accidentally discovers that minerals containing uranium give off invisible rays.

1897

Irene Curie is born. Marie publishes her work on magnets.

Invisible rays

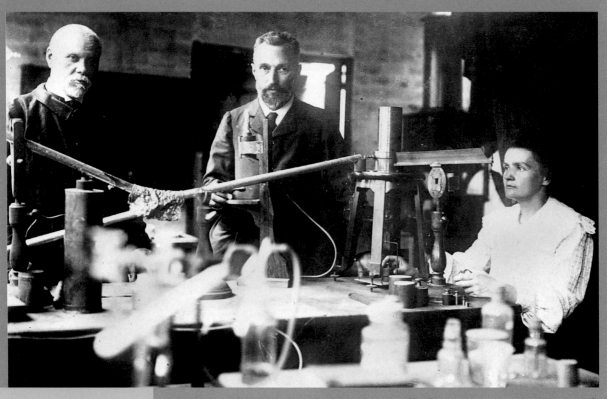

Pierre and Marie used a machine called an electrometer, invented by Pierre several years earlier, to measure the invisible rays.

1898

Marie starts work on her doctorate. Pierre starts to work alongside Marie. They test various minerals and discover that pitchblende gives off more invisible rays than minerals containing uranium.

Looking for a subject for her next degree, Marie became fascinated by the invisible rays that the scientist, Henri Becquerel, had accidentally discovered two years earlier. Soon Pierre joined Marie, working with her to measure the strength of the invisible rays that came off uranium and other minerals.

1898

They discovered that the mineral, pitchblende, gave off rays four times stronger than those coming from minerals containing uranium. But which part, or element, of pitchblende was giving off the rays?

EXPLAINING ELEMENTS

Elements are made of tiny building blocks, or particles, called atoms. The atoms of one element are different to the atoms of another element. There are over a hundred different types of element. Gold is an element and pure gold is only made up of atoms of gold.

Marie was given use of a shed for her experiments.

Discovery!

Pierre and Marie became certain that the invisible rays were coming from a new, radioactive element within pitchblende. They called the element polonium, after Poland. Two weeks later they announced the discovery of another new element, radium. In order to prove their discoveries, they needed to separate the new elements from all the rest of the elements within pitchblende.

Marie and Pierre in their laboratory.

1898

Sack loads of pitchblende arrive at the Curies' research shed. Pierre's father looks after Irene who rarely sees her parents.

July 1898

The Curies announce the discovery of the element, polonium.

December 1898

They announce the discovery of another new element, radium.

1898–1903

It was Marie who did most of the hard work, crushing the pitchblende, dissolving it in acid and boiling it up. She repeated experiments over and over again, writing the results in notebooks. Finally, Marie and Pierre had extracted one tenth of a gram of radium, their new element, and it gave off a greenish glow.

Day after day Marie boiled up huge pans of pitchblende, as imagined by this artist.

BREAKTHROUGH

Pitchblende is made up of about 30 different elements. The Curies knew that it only contained a tiny amount of the radioactive elements they were searching for. By processing 8,000 kilograms of it over the course of four years, they extracted enough radium to prove its existence.

September 1898	1901	1902	1903
Marie uses the word 'radioactivity' in a scientific work.	Pierre works with doctors to show that radiation from radium can kill cancer cells.	Marie's father dies. The Curies have one tenth of a gram of radium.	Marie is awarded her doctorate.

15

Nobel Prize and tragedy

Some people could not believe that Marie had done as much of the scientific work as her husband, Pierre.

Many people around the world were extremely excited by the new element, radium, but no one realised how dangerous it could be. Marie and Pierre often felt tired and ill but they did not know the cause. Despite their ill health, Marie and Pierre were overjoyed when they received a Nobel Prize in 1903 for discovering radium.

1903	1904	1904	1906
The Nobel Prize in Physics is awarded to Henri Becquerel and the Curies for the discovery of radium.	Pierre is made a professor at the Sorbonne.	Eve Curie is born.	Pierre is run over by a horse and carriage.

Just three years later Pierre was killed in an accident. Marie was heartbroken. She cared for her daughters, returned to work and even took on his job at the university but it was a sad time.

Despite a scandal caused by Marie's short love affair with a married man in 1910, she was awarded a second Nobel Prize, this time in chemistry, in 1911.

Marie and her daughters, Eve and Irene.

BREAKTHROUGH

In 1907 Marie made an even purer form of radium. This helped doctors who were using radium and radiation treatments to treat diseases to work out the correct amount to use.

1907	1910	1911	1913
Marie is the first woman professor at the Sorbonne. She makes pure radium.	Her love affair with a married man, Paul Langevin, causes a scandal.	Marie is awarded a second Nobel Prize – in chemistry.	The Curie family go on holiday with Albert Einstein.

War work

August 1914

The Radium Institute building is finished. The First World War breaks out.

Marie decided to devote the rest of her life to science. She became the head of the new Radium Institute in Paris but just as the building was finished, the First World War began. Marie soon realised that doctors could not treat injured soldiers properly because the French army only had one X-ray machine.

October 1914

The first twenty 'petite Curie' vans are in use at the battlefront.

1914–1919

Marie also sets up 200 X-ray units in military hospitals and trains people to work the machines. Marie and Irene receive high doses of radiation as they work without protective clothing.

Marie drove one of the X-ray vans during the war.

1914-1919

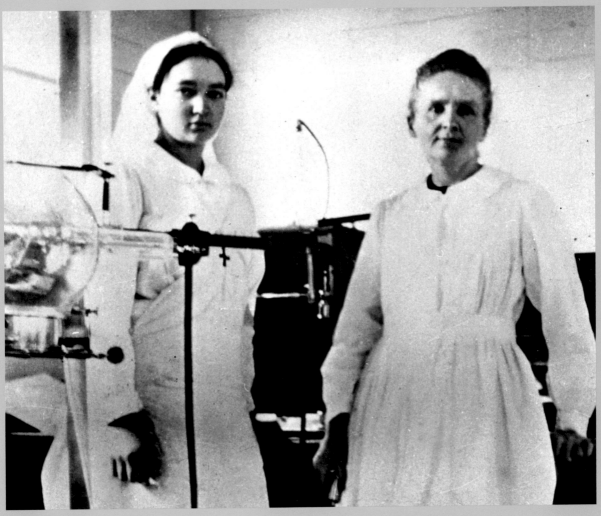

*Marie Curie pictured with her daughter Irene in 1915
when they both worked as nurses during the First World War.*

Marie worked non-stop to persuade people to give money
and equipment to change some cars into vans, each containing
an X-ray machine. The X-ray units were used to treat over a
million wounded soldiers during the war, allowing doctors
to see bullets, shrapnel and broken bones.

Fund-raising trips

After the war, Marie returned to her work at the Radium Institute but she was always short of money and radium. To get more support for the Institute and its work, she agreed to allow an American journalist to write an article about her work. This led to an eight-week tour of the United States.

Marie and her daughters, Irene (left) and Eve (right), during the tour of the United States.

1920

Marie is short of money as the Curies did not take out patents on their discoveries but shared the information for the benefit of all.

1920

Mrs Meloney, a journalist, writes an article about Marie Curie and her work for an American newspaper.

The tour made Marie and her work well known in the United States. It ended with a very special meeting with the President of the United States. He gave her a box containing radium, a gift from the American people to help Marie continue her research. She returned in 1929 to receive money to buy more radium.

Marie met with President Harding of the United States.

1921

Mrs Meloney organises an eight-week tour of the USA to raise money for Marie's research work.

1927

The world's greatest scientists, including Marie, meet to discuss physics.

1929

Marie visits the USA to collect a gift of money to buy radium for the new Radium Institute in Warsaw, Poland.

Her name lives on

Marie continued to work on radium and radiation. However, she began to feel increasingly unwell, due to working with radiation much of her life. It was only during the 1920s that people gradually realised the dangers of working with radium, which destroys blood cells and can cause cancer. Marie's daughters cared for her in the last years of her life.

A portrait of Marie Curie in 1934, at the end of her life.

1932

The Warsaw Radium Institute opens.

1934

Irene and her husband, Frederic Joliot, discover artificial radioactivity, for which they receive a Nobel Prize.

4 July 1934

Marie dies, aged 67. She is buried with her husband Pierre.

1930–today

Marie remains an inspiration to scientists today through her scientific work and her achievements. She discovered not one element, but two, and is the only person to have received the Nobel Prize in Physics and in Chemistry. Her work on radium and radiation led to new treatments for cancer and many other discoveries.

Irene Curie and her husband Frederic Joliot were awarded the Nobel Prize for chemistry in 1935.

1944

A newly discovered radioactive element is named after Pierre and Marie Curie.

1995

The bodies of Marie and Pierre Curie are moved to the Panthéon in Paris, where the greatest French people are honoured.

Glossary

cancer A serious illness that is caused by cells in the body growing in a way that is not normal.

doctorate The highest degree a university can award.

element A substance made up of only one type of atom.

governess A female teacher who teaches children in their own home.

mineral A solid substance that is made up of material (elements) that has never been alive.

Nobel Prize An international prize awarded to scientists, writers or leaders for their outstanding work.

patent A patent establishes ownership of a new discovery or invention.

pitchblende A mined rock made up of over 30 different elements.

polonium A radioactive element discovered by Marie Curie.

radiation Invisible rays given off by radioactive materials.

radioactive Giving off radiation.

radium A radioactive element that glows faintly in the dark.

tuberculosis A serious disease that can usually be cured today.

typhus An infectious disease which causes a rash, aches and sickness or diarrhoea.

X-rays Electromagnetic rays – these pass through most parts of the human body, but not bones or teeth.

Index

atoms 13

Becquerel, Henri 11, 12, 16

cancer 15, 22–23
childhood 4–6
Curie, Bronia 4, 7–9
Curie, Eve 16, 17, 22
Curie, Irene 11, 14, 17, 18, 19, 22–23
Curie, Pierre 10–17

education 5–10
elements 13–16, 23

First World War 18–19

governess (work as a) 7–8

ill health 16, 22

Joliot, Frederic 22, 23

magnets (work on) 10–11
marriage 10–16
Meloney, Mrs 20–21
minerals 11–15

Nobel Prizes 16–17, 22, 23

Panthéon, the 23
'petite Curie' vans 18–19
pitchblende 12–15
polonium 14
President Harding 21
professor (at Sorbonne) 17

radium 14–23
Radium Institute 18, 20–22
Rontgen, Wilhelm 10

Sorbonne University 8–10, 16, 17

uranium 11–13
USA, tours of 20–21

X-rays 10, 18–19